The Sales Operations Handbook

A Primer on the Sales Operations Function

by

WW Chee

Books by
WW Chee

The Sales Operations Handbook

Getting the Most Out of your CRM

Sales Operations for Small Businesses

Managing the Sales Pipeline

Table of Contents

Legal Notes	6
Introduction	7
Chapter 1: The Role of Sales Operations	9
Primary Functions	10
Secondary Functions	11
The Sales Operations Team	11
The Sales Operations Professional	13
Primary Functions	15
Chapter 2: Method	16
Sales methodologies	16
Sales Processes	21
Chapter 3: Enablement	24
Sales Process Adoption and Compliance - a Change Management Process	24
Sales Training	27
Mentorship	29
Communicating to your Salespeople	29
Chapter 4: Analysis	31
Leading and Lagging Indicators	31
Leading indicators	32
Lagging indicators	32
Forecasting	33
A method of sales forecasting	34
Variations	34
CAGR	35
Seasonality	35

Actual + Forecast	35
Sales Pipeline Management	**35**
Sales Pipeline and the CRM	38
Sales Capacity Planning	38
Sales Portfolio planning	39
Compensation Planning	41
Secondary Functions	**42**
Chapter 5: Sales Tools	**43**
Playbooks	44
CRM	45
Sales Performance Management	45
CPQ & Contract Management	46
Business Intelligence	46
BI Tools & Sales Operations	47
Templates &Collateral	47
Chapter 6: Sales Administration	**49**
Proposal Development	49
Contract Processing	50
Vendor Selection and Management	50
Chapter 7: Future Trends	**52**
A More Strategic Role	52
Technology	53
Big Data	53
Data Security	55
Sales Operations as a Service	55
Appendix I: Case Study	**57**
Why Sales Operations Management Makes a Difference in a Business Organization	57
What is Sales Operations Management?	57

What Does Sales Operations Management Address? 57
How Does Sales Operations Management Work? 59
The Results of Company X's Sales Operation
    Management Efforts 64
Summing It All Up 66

Legal Notes

Copyright 2017 - All rights reserved

This document contains opinions and ideas of the author. It is sold for the purpose of providing helpful and reliable information; the publish, author, and all other parties involved in the making of this document are not required to render any qualified services or advice.

The information provided herein is strictly for educational purposes; any liability, in terms of inattention or otherwise, by any usage or abuse of any policies, processes, or directions contained within, is the solitary and utter responsibility of the reader.

Under no circumstances will any legal responsibility or blame be held against the publisher, author, or any other parties involved in the making of this document for any reparation, damages, or monetary loss due to the information herein, either directly or indirectly.

Permission is not granted to reproduce, duplicate, or transmit any part of this document in electronic or printed format. Recording of this publication is also prohibited and storage of this document is not allowed without the written permission from the publisher. All rights are reserved.

Introduction

In recent times, sales organizations have become more reliant on analysis and processes, due to the scope of data readily available, which has led to an impetus for change in the way sales are carried out. Where sales operations were once measuring the productivity of salespeople, we are now generating opportunities and shortening the lead response time even as sales is becoming more complex.

Xerox pioneered the role of sales operations in the 1970's and, since the turn of the 21st century, more and more organizations have implemented sales operations functions, including Microsoft, Google, LinkedIn, Samsung, Thomson Reuters and Verizon. However, with any nascent function there is confusion surrounding the role and purpose of sales operations and its place in the business organization.

The main function of the sales operations team is to smoothen the sales process by removing inefficiencies and optimizing the sales function to ensure the successful execution of the organization's sales strategy. This is not to be confused with Sales & Operations, which is unique to the manufacturing industry and is the discipline of optimizing your supply chain with regards to production and sales.

In the past, sales operations were mainly an administrative department; relegated to the function of reporting, and number crunching. Now, it is more common for sales operations to be a strategic partner, helping to make sense of data and interpret the results.

I have often explained my role in sales operations to friends and family by oversimplifying it as "everything sales management would do except directly interacting with a customer." I have spent over 10 years working in the sales operations department in global MNCs and have performed all the functions related to the discipline mentioned in this e-Book. Sales operations is a fairly new career path and resources are fairly lacking. Hence I have gathered my knowledge and put it down in here.

To help you understand sales operation, I identify and define the array of functions a sales operations team is responsible for in this e-Book. If you are considering a career, or have just started a role in sales operations, this is meant to be a primer for your journey.

This book is for you.

Chapter 1: The Role of Sales Operations

Wikipedia defines sales operations is a set of business activities and processes that help a sales organization run effectively, efficiently and in support of business strategies and business objectives.

Since the early 2000's, more and more companies are forming sales operations departments within their organizations to establish sales processes, monitor sales metrics, and implement the usage of sales tools.

However, with more tools in use, it is estimated that salespeople spend roughly a third of their time selling and the other two-thirds on non-selling activities. It is the sales operations department's job to improve that ratio.

A good sales operations team will have an impact on productivity and increase the effectiveness of salespeople by reducing the time they spend on non-sales tasks, allowing them to spend more time selling. Studies have found that there is a direct correlation between the focus on sales operations and sales target achievements.

While the details may differ from company to company, the scope of the Sales Operations team fall into three primary functions, and two secondary functions.

Primary Functions

1. Method
2. Enablement
3. Analysis

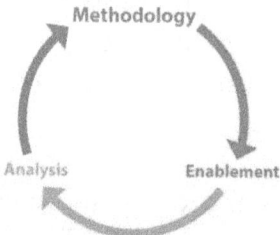

The three primary functions are effectively a cycle.

Methodology is the backbone of the sales organization and determines how the organization sells to its customers. A good methodology that is well implemented will allow the sales organization to have a standardized approach to sales, with a standardized language.

When the method is decided, the salespeople need to be enabled. Enablement is about selecting the right tools, communicating the decisions to the salespeople, and training the salespeople on the usage of the tools, or the purpose of the process.

After the enablement comes the Analysis. KPIs should be defined clearly, and tracked, either via the tools, or from the other departments like operations, or finance. Good analysis should measure the success of the salespeople, and the effectiveness of processes, training, campaigns and all sales activities.

From there it feeds back into the cycle, and sales operations can determine the value of the method and recommend changes to the processes or plans.

Secondary Functions

1. Administration
2. Sales Tools

The secondary functions of the sales operations team are an offshoot of the primary functions. Administrative tasks such as contract filing, order processing, pricing, and upkeep of customer records. This should also be in line with the method, and enablement efforts.

The selection, maintenance, and administration of sales tools also fall under secondary responsibilities. It is usually for the sales operations team to perform data uploads to the tools and provide login details or password resets (or at least arrange with the vendor for the above).

We will look more at the primary and secondary functions of the sales operations team in the chapters ahead.

The Sales Operations Team

Sales operations exist almost exclusively in large organizations and fall outside the traditional corporate culture due to its lack of direct impact on decisions; their recommendations (along with data) are given to the head of sales, who has the final say. The sales operations department is in effect the "Chief of Staff" for the sales organization.

In the past, sales operations have often been considered to bea cost center, where the impact of the team is difficult to calculate, but since organizations are realizing that the sales cycles are getting more complex, and the volume of data available is increasing exponentially, the value of the function cannot be denied when the sales operations team moves from an administrative role to a strategic one.

The goal of the sales operations team is to improve sales performance. This is done by a two-pronged approach. Firstly, sales operations reduce inefficiencies, allowing the salespeople to increase their time in the field selling, by reducing their time spent on other tasks such as generating proposals or presentations. Secondly, sales operations increase the skill of salespeople through enablement, allowing them to improve their effectiveness.

For a large organization with a workforce spread over different locations, improving on systems, data, and analysis would make it easier to align focus and goals. Centralizing the above around a strategy, the sales operations team ensures that the systems are part of the process; having established processes increases the speed a sales opportunity moves through the stages of a sales funnel, by ensuring salespeople understand what needs to be done and in what order. This improves the overall efficiency of the salespeople.

Lastly by establishing best practices in processes, the sales operations team provides top down support to the salespeople as a center of excellence. Ownership of templates and collateral will allow the sales operations team to capture and share best practices among the salespeople.

The Sales Operations Professional

As a sales operations professional, the core function of your role is to improve the efficiency of the sales organization.

Cross-functional experience is highly prized, as very often it is necessary for you to partner with IT, Marketing, and Finance departments to align the sales organization with the goals of the other departments in the organization. Sales operations managers have come from various backgrounds; sales, operations, finance, marketing, and even from consulting. Their value tends to be the skills that they bring to the table.

A background in a quantitative field is often preferred, and a strong affinity with numbers is almost compulsory. As sales operations collect huge amounts of data, it will be your job to derive insights from the data and come up with plans and solutions that will ultimately benefit the sales organization.

The skills required to succeed as a sales operations professional, include an understanding of sales skills, advanced negotiation, a familiarity with reporting metrics, and the ability to implement processes. As you progress in seniority, you will have to develop the ability to influence and handle greater responsibilities. Interpersonal skills, particularly when presenting technical content to general audiences, is useful here.

As a sales operations professional, you will need to be able to operate at a tactical and a strategic level. You will have almost complete visibility of the sales organization and will need to be able to identify gaps in the organization. It is your job to propose solutions to address those gaps. Some examples would be identifying trends in cross-selling, factors that influence proposal win rates, and availability of sales collateral to name a few.

Last but not least, you should be the resident expert on technology such as Customer Relationship Management (CRM) tools, and Business Intelligence (BI) tools, since in most organizations sales operations have ownership of these.

Primary Functions

Chapter 2: Method

Method is the procedure and system of sales. It is guided by the organization's vision and the objective of the sales department. It encompasses the methodology, which defines the organization's overall approach to sales, and the process which is the step by step guide on how to move a sale forward.

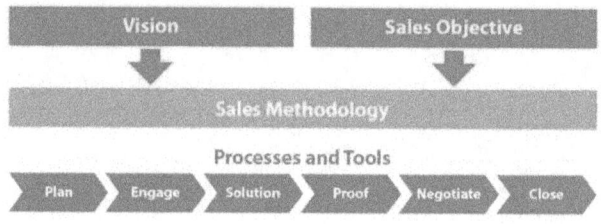

Sales methodologies

A sales methodology to sales operations is like an operating system (e.g. Windows or Linux) to a computer. It defines the language, the drivers, and the "how" of selling to customers.

The purpose of a sales methodology is to drive sales effectiveness and focus the development of sales skills. Having a universal language for sales in the organization is the first step to optimizing sales for the organization.

A universal language removes any ambiguity on terminology, allowing better forecasts, and easier communication when salespeople are requesting support from management. For example, when a salesperson in an organization using Conceptual Selling explains to management why their customer's Economic Buying Influencer (EBI) is not moving the deal forward because of doubts, management would understand the importance of the EBI and how to structure a sales call to the customer.

There are various sales methodologies being used to structure the sales processes in the organization. While the selection of a sales methodology may be decided at a high level, regardless of which methodology an organization chooses to adopt, the enablement and analysis skills required of the sales operations team are equally applicable.

Here is a short summary of some of the popular sales methodologies in use:

Miller-Heiman (Conceptual Selling)
Conceptual Selling was developed by Stephen Heiman and Robert Miller. It focuses on the idea of selling a concept to your buyer, instead of a product. The goal is to discover the concept that the customer is looking for by following a three-step approach:

- Get information: Gather information on the customer such as the organization's needs. It is important to understand what solution the customeris looking for and to find out the problem that they are looking to solve (the concept).

This step is also important in identifying the key stakeholders, their potential role in influencing the sale, and their attitude towards your organization.

- Gain support: After determining the level of support from the stakeholders, the salesperson needs to win the support by understanding what each stakeholder values and help them see how the concept will deliverthat value.

This may be done by linking the customer's needs to the product your organization provides, showing how your solution can help the customer achieve the concept that they have.

- Get commitment: Consistently move the deal forward. This can be done by getting your buyer to commit to the next step (e.g. a demonstration with management, a discussion on technical specifications, a possible trial period, a date for project implementation, etc.)

The use of "Green Sheets," "Blue Sheets" and "Gold Sheets," are a means for salespeople to update their tactical and strategic goals and challenges, and then seek support from their managers.

Challenger Sales

The Challenger Sale is based on the book by Matthew Dixon and Brent Adamson. This model classifies salespeople into 5 types, the most effective of which are the Challengers:

1. Relationship Builders
2. Hard Workers

3. Lone Wolves
4. Problem Solvers
5. Challengers

Dixon and Adamson have identified the approach that makes Challenger salespeople effective. They reduce it to three points which are summarized below:

- Teach: By sharing knowledge on the industry, and how your solution is relevant to the customer, a Challenger shows value and helps the customer to understand more than how your product or solution works. By changing the customer's perspective of their business, the Challenger changes the customer's perspective of your organization.

- Tailor: Challengers often tailor their communications with customers for impact by adjusting their communications based on the customer's value drivers, and their own understanding of the customer's organization. The goal is to have better value based discussions, instead of just imparting knowledge.

- Take control: Challengers take control of the sale by bringing new ideas to the table. The Challenger pushes the customer, convincing them of the urgency of the problem; but in a way that is respectful, and sensitive to their reactions.

Solution Selling

Solution Selling teaches that salespeople should focus less on specific products and more on aligning their selling activities with how customers buy.

Solution Selling has evolved over the years, but it boils down to following these nine steps:

- Prospecting
- Diagnosing customer needs
- Crafting a potential solution
- Establishing value
- Understanding the customer's decision making
- Bargaining for access to decision-makers
- Positioning proof, ROI, and the total solution
- Negotiating a win-win solution
- Following up to ensure customer success

The goal is to build a collaborative relationship with the customer; this is one where they are willing to engage in value-based discussions and trust in your organization's ability to develop solutions.

Customer-Centric Selling

Customer-Centric selling focuses on the customer instead of the usual processes, such as making presentations, convincing your buyer, or offering solutions.

This approach believes the sale is won by having intelligent conversations with key stakeholders, which help customers visualize how to use your organization's product or service. The seven tenets of Customer-Centric Selling are:

1. Have situational conversations

2. Ask relevant questions instead of offering opinions
3. Focus on the solution instead of the relationship
4. Target the stakeholders instead of the users
5. Relate product usage to customer
6. Manage the sale
7. Empower buyers

While the difference in sales methodologies may seem slight, it is their ideologies that set them apart and as a result they each approach sales from a different perspective. Some are geared towards customer acquisition, others towards retention. Some are geared towards large accounts, and others may be better suited to quick turnaround on sales.

It is important to understand the strengths in each methodology and choose or adapt them to your organization's needs. Some organizations may mix and match elements from two or more methodologies, to customize it to their organization. After all, the sales methodology has to be aligned to the organization's vision and sales objectives, and if there is no perfect solution then it makes sense to customize one to fit the organization.

Sales Processes

Where methodologies are the "big picture", sales processes give a step by step stage of the sales cycle for each individual opportunity.

They provide a clear guide on what the salesperson needs to do at each stage, what outcome to expect, and what the next stage is, from prospecting to qualifying, to close. By having a process, it reduces the time salespeople need to think about how to execute on their sales by staying consistent.

A sales process is important for gaining new customers, and planning sales calls through structured engagement.

The sales process should be a collection of best practices for moving the customer through each stage of the process and the desired outcome of each stage. Very often a win/loss analysis of deals feeds back into the modification and evolution of an organization's sales process.

Whichever sales process your organization has adopted, the goal is to have a standardized and repeatable approach to selling, with language that is universally understood in the organization.

From a sales operations perspective, the sales process chosen by the organization will impact how the enablement is carried out, from training to selection of tools, as well as what metrics to keep track of. Administration of proposals, quotations, and lead generation may also feed into the process.

Below is a sample of a sales process, divided into 6 stages. The names and number of stages may vary from organization to organization, and some may even use a flow chart instead.

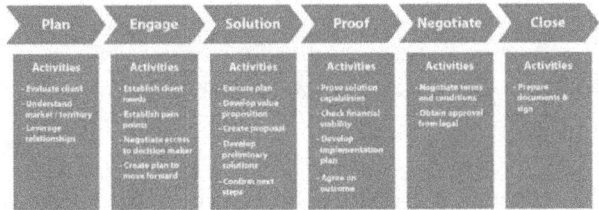

By breaking down the sales process into stages, it allows us to understand which parts are causing inefficiency, while streamlining the process into a few stages allows salespeople to manage each opportunity more effectively.

Chapter 3: Enablement

Sales enablement is generally focused in the pre-engagement and early stages of engagement with the customer.

As sales move further away from a transactional model, and more towards a consultative approach, sales operations play a key role in supporting the salespeople to develop themselves. Sales enablement ensures that the salespeople have access to the necessary knowledge to perform and excel at their jobs.

A sales organization's sales tools and other platforms or applications commonly fall under sales enablement. The main areas of sales enablement are in training, content, sales tools, and sales processes; this also includes selecting and adjusting the above to support the organization's sales strategy.

The goal is to deliver value to the sales team in a flexible and scalable manner. And to do that, sales enablement must select and implement tools that are integrated, robust, and cost-effective.

Sales Process Adoption and Compliance - a Change Management Process

As processes are constantly being accessed, modified, and updated, enablement is a change management process. Ideally, this should be a planned process, rather than a reactive one, and should be tailored to each organization.

It is the responsibility of the sales operations team to prepare the salespeople as they adopt the changes identified by the organization as necessary. This includes equipping them with the appropriate tools such as manuals, and supporting them by providing coaching and reinforcement after training.

There are 4 steps to implementing a change:

1. Identify

The first step of a change management process is identifying what changes will be made, including the resources and people involved that will facilitate the process.

2. Present Business Case

Stakeholders, including upper management, will have different expectations and experiences, and buy-in will be necessary.

The stages from beginning to outcome must be clearly laid out, along with the factors for success and failure. Breaking it down into smaller steps will provide better control of the process and allow successes to be measured more carefully.

3. Implement Change

Identifying, planning, on-boarding, and executing a change management plan requires good communication.

Culture, background, and capabilities of salespeople need to be taken into consideration when implementing change. These factors are the main cause of resistance, which is an inherent part of the process, and arises mainly due to fear of the unknown, and risks (whether real or perceived) associated with the change.

4. Review

As change management is a process, review is essential in adjusting the strategies. Reviews, like communication, should occur constantly and involve all stakeholders, as well as those impacted by the change.

While change management may be a discipline unto itself, there are three key things to note in this aspect with regards to sales operations.

Communication is key. When change occurs, there will inevitably be resistance. This is mainly due to people being removed from their comfort zones. This can be countered by early, constant, and open communication between management, and the people who will be affected by the change.

Feedback is important. When receiving feedback, it is important to understand the underlying concerns of the salespeople. Some of the concerns they bring up may require a new process that should be adopted in a way that is pragmatic to both the salespeople on the frontline and the sales operations team. Other concerns may stem from fears, misinformation, or misunderstanding which should be addressed.

Show the value. While the ultimate goal of the change is usually an improvement on the top or bottom line, the people affected by the change must understand the value that it would bring to them; whether it is a reduction in workload or requests for information, or an improvement in getting support on their tasks. Sell the change to them by explaining what is in it for them as individuals.

Sales Training

As sales move to a more consultative approach, it is becoming more and more important for salespeople to constantly train and update their skills. The development of training curriculum and material is the purview of sales enablement, as is the actual training; both the development and training may be outsourced to vendors while sales operations play a consultative role in the process.With the prevalence of developing technology, it is fairly common for some of this training to be delivered via training portals or employee portals online where feedback and results can be given instantaneously.

Some of the types of training are:

Sales Methodology Training: Understanding the methodologies used by the sales organization increases individual performance and also helps increase predictability in the funnel. By identifying where opportunities are stalling, sales operations can identify where salespeople need help in moving a sale forward.

Market Training: Understanding the market is important for salespeople to bring value and engage their customers in an insightful way. By understanding the market, salespeople are better able to help customers make informed decisions and be seen as an advisor or partner, rather than a vendor. Sales operations should be the source of this information, supplying the data, analysis, and insights to the markets.

Product Training: As products are constantly updated, changed, and launched, salespeople need to constantly improve their skills on product offerings. Product training is focused on the specifications, the facts, and the features of the organization's product offerings. This training is to help salespeople understand the products that they are selling, and be able to address any questions that come up from customers.

Tools Training: When implementing new tools in the organization, it is common for sales operations to conduct training on them, or get the vendors to conduct such a training. It is important the salespeople who will be using the tool understand how they can use it to improve their performance.

On-boarding: This is a type of training given to new hires, usually within their first few months in the organization. On-boarding helps to impart the culture, methods, and processes of the organization into the new hire as early as possible, to improve adoption and learning.

Internal certification from sales training is a practice that ensures a minimum competency of salespeople and may be broken down into basic, intermediate, and advanced levels. Each certification level could define a certain mastery or different level of the above training.

Mentorship

Mentorship is a common practice in organizations to groom the next generation of leadership; by setting up a formal program, sales operations can ensure a transfer of skills, culture, best practices, and knowledge to emerging sales leaders.

Successful mentorship programs expose participants with different managers at senior levels and retain internal talent.

Along with an on-boarding training, a mentoring program will also help new hires to integrate with the organization at a quicker rate, as they have someone to help them understand the organization's culture.

Communicating to your Salespeople

Having a channel to communicate with all your salespeople is useful in disseminating critical information.

E-newsletters, announcements, and updates, are essential platforms to reinforce processes, highlight best practices, and encourage compliance to new procedures.

These platforms are also useful in celebrating wins, which can serve to positively reinforce the above. Salespeople who adopt best practices set forth by the wins may produce success stories of their own.

This aspect, while often overlooked in my experience, is an essential tool in helping salespeople learn from each other, and improves interaction which leads to a reinforcement of culture by underlining a sense of team belonging.

Chapter 4: Analysis

While the role of the sales operations analyst centers around reports, sales modelling, and spreadsheets in general, there is a trend that is moving the job scope towards generating business insights. Data visualization such as dashboards, charts, and PowerPoint slides are focused around a situation or issue, and how the impact of that affects the organization.

For example, a decline in sales in a certain territory or market segment may be dueto a shift in customer preference towards a competitor or a new product. Such insight could lead to management deciding the best course of action to take to retain existing customers, or whether refocusing their attention elsewhere might be a better course of action (depending on business strategy).

It is also the sales operation's job to select the data to track what is relevant, to help management understand the activities within the organization. This would result in management being able to make well informed decisions. To do this, they generate regular reports and ensure this data is clean, accurate, and complete.

Leading and Lagging Indicators

When dealing with reports, there are two kinds of inputs:

1. Today's numbers that show the metrics for the future, the leading indicators
2. Historic numbers that show the performance of the past, the lagging indicators

Each of them has their uses and should be used situationally.

Leading indicators

Leading indicators are used to predict changes in sales, and are usually input oriented. They measure the activities needed to achieve sales goals and estimate how likely it is that the sales goal will be achieved.

CRM tools, sales funnel stages, pipeline volume, and associated metrics are a good source of leading indicators. These metrics will give an expectation of the performance of the organization in the future.

By measuring the number of sales calls, open opportunities, and proposals submitted, sales operations are making an educated guess on the future sales figures.

A word of caution that leading indicators comes from the input of salespeople. While the sales methodology and sales process should ensure the language used is universal, there is still some element of gut feel to metrics in the pipeline. Leading indicators such as expected close dates and expected volume are especially vulnerable to this, so do not count your chickens before they hatch.

Lagging indicators

Lagging indicators are used to assess the past performance of the organization, and are usually output oriented. Some examples are customer visits, revenue, and units sold.

With the advent of business intelligence tools, there is a large amount of data available in any organization. Figures such as sales volume, revenue and margins, among others, should be easily available.

These metrics will give an update on the historic performance of the organization in a given period. It is common for analysis to be run for seasonality, market share, year on year comparisons, or a combination of the above.

The value of lagging indicators is that it allows us insight into how the organization has performed compared to our forecasts. Either too high or low, and there may be a mismatch between capability and expectation.

Forecasting

Sales operations are essential in producing reports and analysis which drive recommendations. By using predictive models, the sales operations department can help take an active role in closing the gap between expected and actual sales performance.

Accurate sales forecasts allow companies to make informed business decisions, such as product launches, headcount needs, cash flow, and other resource allocations.

A method of sales forecasting

The first step is to look at the expected account growth or closure of existing customers. Are there a number of accounts that shut down each period? Is there an organic growth in the business of your customers, which would result in increased sales? That should be accounted for to get the base, which is the status quo, without the impact of salespeople.

Secondly, we would need to factor in the efforts of our own salespeople. This would be the growth due to new customers, contracts won, or increased orders from existing customers. This may be done by comparing the previous period of sales with the current period, and extrapolating the data based upon the growth rates calculated.

Thirdly, we put steps one and two together. The organic growth plus sales effort would give us the expected sales for the forecast period.

From experience, this process may be repeated several times throughout the year and each forecast may have several iterations as growth rates and targets are debated. It pays to remember that a forecast is only as reliable as the data that goes into it, and is only as effective when they are realistic.

Variations

There are a few slight variations to how organizations might do their forecasts.

CAGR

Some organizations may prefer to use the Compound Annual Growth Rates (CAGR) instead and forecast the current year's performance by applying the CAGR to previous year's performance of sales.

Seasonality

Some organizations have their sales in cycles. Whether it is years, months, or quarters, these organizations see a pattern to their sales and take into account a seasonality to their forecast.

Actual + Forecast

Aside from the annual, quarterly, and monthly forecasts, some organizations practice using the actual year to date performance and then apply the forecast to the rest of the year. For example, using a calendar year in April the organization might do a 4+8 forecast. Meaning 4 months of actual sales, with 8 months of forecast sales.

Sales Pipeline Management

The sales pipeline pulls together all sales prospects and the stages that each opportunity is in and presents this in a visual manner.

Pipelines provide an overview of a salesperson's, sales team's, or entire organization's accounts, and gives a forecast of how close a team is to reaching their sales goals based on the conversion rates for each of the stages of the funnel.

The stages should be clearly defined in the sales process (see Chapter 2), with a language that is commonly understood by everyone in the sales organization.

By agreeing on the stages and the language, a sales culture is developed. Terms would be clearly defined in a playbook, or at least in the sales process, which would remove any ambiguity on what each stage of the sales pipeline means. This ultimately improves the flow through rate of opportunities in the pipeline as salespeople using the process become more proficient in using it.

While many of these opportunities may also be reflected in the forecast, care should be taken in selecting those only in the final stages for consideration. There is always a possibility that an opportunity might be lost before closing.

Some common metrics when reviewing the funnel are:

- Number of deals in the pipeline
- Average deal size
- Conversion rate - % chance that a deal moves to the next pipeline stage
- Average time spent in each stage of the pipeline

By having the above, it is common for sales operations to review the pipeline with salespeople on a regular basis, to understand what is happening with a deal. Usually, only major deals are tracked but often sales operations look at the pipeline as a whole.

Some common questions to ask when reviewing the pipeline are:

- How many opportunities were won and lost in the period?

Understanding the win/loss ratio helps to determine the success of the sales process and the skill of the salespeople.

- At what stage of the pipeline did the opportunities drop out?

Which stage opportunities drop out of the pipeline will show where the weaknesses of the salespeople are. Is the organization losing out in product features or price? Or perhaps it is the salesperson's presentations that need to be upgraded?

- Are there any opportunities that have been at a stage in the pipeline for a long period?

Stale opportunities show a lack of engagement with the customer. There is a risk that such customers may end up going to a competitor, resulting in a lost sale. If the opportunity is left at a stage by the salesperson, they might have too many accounts in their portfolio. If the customer is stalling, then perhaps a follow up visit is required.

- What is the volume in terms of sales, or revenue, at each stage of the pipeline?

Too low a volume would indicate more leads are necessary. Too large a volume in a stage would suggest that focus might be needed to clear a large deal or a large volume of deals.

By looking at the above, it helps to focus management's attention on the customers that are most likely to close, and understand the factors involved in swaying a customer's decision. Forecasting on the leading indicators from the funnel also gives some predictability to the sales process.

Sales Pipeline and the CRM

CRM systems supplement the sales pipeline by allowing the sales teams to track their opportunities, and automate the sales process. It also allows sales operations to monitor the health of the funnel, and manage the sales organization.

Sales Capacity Planning

For salespeople to fulfill their individual targets, and by extension their team targets, it is necessary to balance between output and employee turnover. By measuring and predicting the performance of salespeople, we can optimize the sales capacity of the organization.

Capacity Planning breaks down goals into monthly targets, and through the pipeline stages of your organization's chosen sales methodology.

This is done by quantifying the performance of each individual salesperson, based on their number of sales calls, sales volumes, and close rates. The benefit of this is to manage headcount, and sales performance to match the opportunities in the market ensuring that there are no untargeted opportunities due to insufficient salespeople or vice-versa, an excess of salespeople with insufficient opportunities.

It should be noted that different salespeople have different strengths, and may be better suited for different markets or products. Calculating the win rates for each salesperson allows us to understand the type of opportunities they are best able to handle. For example, some salespeople might be better at maintaining existing customers while others may excel at pitching to a competitor's customer.

Sales enablement can also improve the performance of salespeople, increasing their capacity by giving them a better understanding of the methodology, processes, and tools through training.

Sales Portfolio planning

Sales portfolio planning is done to strategize the sales and territories in the market. This is done to protect and grow revenue as well as customer loyalty, and also to tailor individual portfolios to the capacity of the sales organization. A well-managed sales portfolio plan will keep the cost of sales under control by effectively allocating salespeople to clients.

1. Segment your clients
2.

Whether it is by industry, geography, product, or business unit, grouping clients will allow your sales teams to specialize.

This also allows for customers to be analysed by segment; forecasting can be adjusted based on industry trends, or geographical factors. Sales operations can also understand how each segment is performing according to plan, and take steps if necessary to remedy the situation.

3. Identify top clients in each segment

Very often the 80/20 rule (aka Pareto Principle) applies to account planning. This means a large portion of an organization's sales comes from a few key clients. By servicing these clients well, and retaining their business, the organization would have a steady amount of revenue base.

4. Target clients in each segment

Growth in sales usually comes from winning new clients, or from switching over clients from your competitors. It falls to sales operations to identify these potential clients (with the input from salespeople), and devise a plan of action in capturing this revenue segment.

Planning the portfolio of your salespeople will enhance customer coverage by ensuring that the accounts are spread across the sales organization's workforce. Accounts that are unassigned, or fall by the wayside due to a high volume of customers in an individual salesperson's portfolio can be easily reassigned. This ensures that the organization does not miss out on any opportunities that may have been otherwise left undiscovered.

Proper distribution of the sales territories may also align salesperson incentives. High value clients, or possibly easy accounts, may be concentrated in an individual's portfolio and may result in certain individuals seemingly outperforming their colleagues. Portfolio planning will allow the organization to understand the true potential of their salespeople better, instead of handing out incentives based purely upon the nature of an individual's portfolio.

Compensation Planning

Since sales operations monitor sales activities closely linked with capacity planning and account planning, some organizations involve sales operations in compensation planning as well.

It is common to have finance or HR handle the payments and communication of the plan, developing and measuring the success of it with the input of sales operations, if not by the sales operations department itself.

The mix of accounts of a salesperson, the sales cycle and the number of people involved in a sale will all affect the structuring of a compensation plan. Sales operations, with their availability of such data, are positioned to provide expert advice on this.

Another area of sales that compensation is involved in, is the governance of the compensation plan. While the plan will most likely not cover all possible scenarios, details over how conflicts will be resolved should be put in place. A committee may be formed to deal with any such situations, or sometimes it may default to the discretion of the head of sales.

With that said, there is a common adage that "you get what you incentivize." Compensation plans tend to influence the behavior of the salespeople, which may sometimes conflict with the organization's best interests. For example, incentivizing based upon market share may result in salespeople preferring to be "farmers" where they service existing accounts, instead of prospecting for new clients.

Secondary Functions

Chapter 5: Sales Tools

Sales tools are the materials, systems, and resources available to the salespeople, to help them improve their sales. The best sales teams are equipped with the tools and technologies that will help achieve their sales goals and drive their success.

When choosing sales tools, the goal again is efficiency. A tool must fill a gap in the organization, improving an area where salespeople need to be faster, better, or more efficient by focusing on the right things. To do this the purpose of the tool needs to be considered; the impact of the technology is more important than the functionality of the tool.

Tools that are chosen must be well integrated; double entry of data, lack of data sharing or updates, inability to port the data to a dashboard or export it to a spreadsheet are common issues that would hinder salespeople and cancel out any potential time savings the tools would bring.

Scalability should also be considered. The number of users, additional products, or even business lines have to be able to scale with the organization's future plans.

These are some tools that are used in organizations to help sales operations achieve their goals. This list is not exhaustive, and the individual tool or software may vary from company to company.

Playbooks

A playbook is the go-to resource for salespeople, created by the sales operations team, sometimes in conjunction with marketing.

It is usually launched in conjunction with the organization's chosen sales methodology or sales process. The playbook should ideally enhance the awareness and educate all salespeople on the value of the sales methodology, sales process, and tools at their disposal.

It is a reference to ensure that the salespeople understand how the organization sells, and the role that they play, along with the expected outcomes in each stage of the sales process.

A good playbook should:

- Define the sales methodology and sales process
- Map the sales process to the customer's buying process
- Guide the engagement with a prospective customer
- State the tools, resources and outcome of each stage of the sales process
- Contain an explanation of resources and tools available to salespeople

Due to the above, playbooks are also a good resource to help new hires acclimatize to the culture of the organization.

CRM

This is the most commonly encountered tool in sales operations. A good Customer Relationship Management (CRM) tool enables the organization to record, improve, and consistently service their customers.

By having salespeople record their sales visits and calls, along with outcomes, it is possible to better understand the capability of the sales team, the market, and each segmentation. This in turn allows for better capacity planning, development of resources, and analysis. Ultimately the relationship with the customer improves, resulting in increased customer loyalty and improved sales.

The CRM can also be used to record sales visits and calls to prospective clients. In this case, tracking the engagement, and understanding where the sales person is in the sales process with the customer.

Implementing a CRM system should ideally give better coordination on interaction with the customer, improved management visibility on sales person activity, and the ability to tailor the sales approach to the customer.

Sales Performance Management

Sales Performance Management (SPM) tools track the performance of the sales organization and guide the salespeople to improve their effectiveness in the field. SPM tools assist in the sales performance management process and streamline activities to encourage behaviors that drive sales.

SPM tools very often include features that track data, such as sales quotas, achievements, incentives, and forecasts. These tools also benefit salespeople by helping them set relevant goals and track their performance against them.

CPQ & Contract Management

Configure Price Quote (CPQ) tools are software designed to help salespeople quote for complex, configurable products and ensure a more consistent quotation to the customer, in a shorter time period, with fewer errors.

By factoring in the choices in the configuration of the product (or service), the pricing is then adjusted to sell the product as a bundle, taking into account all costs such as geography, regulations, competitors and such.

Thus, CPQ tools should allow salespeople to make more informed quotations to their customers, and respond quickly and more effectively to any changes in their requirements.

Business Intelligence

Business Intelligence (BI) software is a type of application software designed to leverage on data and convert it to information to drive analysis.

With the large amount of data available in this age, BI tools are needed to deliver the right information to the right person at the right time.

Spreadsheets, data mining, data visualization, and dashboards are examples of BI tools. CRM and CPQ tools may also contain a BI element to them in their reporting functions.

Selecting the proper BI tools will improve the quality of data, which in turn improves the quality of analysis. This provides more relevant insights to management which can be acted upon, to ultimately improve sales.

Automating reports and dashboards would eliminate, or at least reduce, the need to create complex spreadsheets, and likely even remove errors and inconsistent data since similar reports will be pulled using the same tool and using the same predefined calculations. Where several teams of analysts may once be required to generate reports, they are now primarily tasks with analysing data for insights.

BI Tools & Sales Operations

When dealing with BI tools, sales operations would need to enable by ensuring a right selection of tools, integrating it into the sales process, and training salespeople to use them.

Additionally, sales operations need to leverage on the data of these tools for analysis. The value of BI tools is ultimately in the insights it can bring to the sales organization and the sales or efficiencies it can generate as a result.

Templates &Collateral

In organizations, it is common for salespeople to develop documents such as case studies, email templates, cold call scripts, contracts, proposals, and product information mailers. This results in having different standards for documents, where some may be better developed than others. Even if this is developed by a department, not everyone may be updated with the latest version of documents.

Sales operations can step in to manage this by ensuring access to a document library. A shared drive or intranet portal may be used to actively manage this. By ensuring the custodianship of templates and collateral, old documents are constantly updated and new documents are more readily available throughout the organization.

Chapter 6: Sales Administration

Part of the sales operations portfolio is administrating the day-to-day activities of the sales organization. While it may seem mundane and monotonous, a smooth flow in administration ensures faster turnaround on other sales operations activities.

Proposal Development

With the pace of business increasing in spite of deals being more complex, it is important that sales operations provide the sales team with high-quality proposals that can be turned around quickly and efficiently. These proposals must be positioned competitively; in addition, they must also fulfil customer objectives and establish mutual value between the customer and the organization.

It is common for sales operations to maintain a contracts library to file previously submitted contracts and proposals for reference. Notes on the outcome, along with customer testimonials may also be included for future use.

Having templates, scripts, and content will assist salespeople to communicate with prospects, and guide them along the sales process, reducing their time spent on creating or looking for material.

Contract Processing

The time between closing the deal and the signing of documents is a risk period. Any negative experience during these first few moments will impact the rest of the relationship. Sales operations can enable this process by having the right template of contracts in a contract library (mentioned above).

An electronic signature or digital transaction tool may also be used to shorten the contract processing time by managing document-centric business processes. These tools reduce the friction inherent in transactions that involve people, documentation, and data, by using electronic means instead of manual paper processes.

Having a process in contract management will also smoothen this process and remove any obstacles beforehand.

Vendor Selection and Management

Vendor management for sales operations usually includes the CRM system, BI tools, and corporate trainers. This may also extend to the hiring process, lead generation, or any other activity that can be outsourced.

For example, having a contingent workforce to support your salespeople will ensure that they have the required resources as necessary while keeping headcount low during high seasons, trade fairs, conferences, or other such activities which vary from industry to industry.

Sales operations are able to determine which functions of the sales organization to map prospective vendors against the organization's sales processes and needs, by identifying gaps in processes and then mapping each vendor's offerings to impact in salespeople efficiency.

The vendor selection process starts with understanding the organization's needs that will be addressed by the vendor. Ideally, a solution or type of solution will be identified at this stage and exploration can begin.

The next step is to identify vendors that are able to supply the solutions identified. Characteristics like geography, support, costs, and features need to be taken into account. It is common for a request for proposal (RFP) or a direct engagement with a vendor to happen with multiple vendors.

Once proposals have been sent it, they need to be reviewed to ensure that the solution offered fits into the organization's goals, and can fulfil the organization's needs before short listing and selecting the winning vendor.

Chapter 7: Future Trends

As more and more companies form sales operations departments, the role of sales operations is slowly but surely being defined. From sales operations blogs, conferences, and workforce mobility, best practices are being pollinated across sales operations departments. However, the rapid development and deployment of technology will be the main driving factor behind many of these.

Currently, there are a few trends that are beginning to emerge.

A More Strategic Role

Where sales operations were previously an administrative or a reporting function they are now moving towards optimizing sales.

Internally, the encompassing purview of method, enablement, and analysis, sales operations is empowered to reduce inefficient processes in the sales organization. Processes which are supported by tools are streamlined, becoming more efficient and allow salespeople more time on the field.

Externally, market research into untapped segments of the customer base, cross-selling of products between lines of businesses, increasing customer retention through regular engagement, future planning, and projection of revenue are just some examples of what is possible.

Focusing on the internal and external drivers above, sales operations are able to support management in linking the tactical aspects of sales to the organization's strategic goals.

Technology

With the surge in the popularity of smart phones, the usage of mobile apps has seen a sharp increase. This puts tools like CRM, analytics, customer portals, and others in the palms of all salespeople.

Information is more widely available, which would shorten turnaround time. Salespeople are able toaccess information such as the purchase history, last engagement, and annual spend of customers in short order as sales tools move to a mobile platform.

The value of this is not to be underestimated.With this technology, the prospect of understanding and engaging the customer with the same amount of preparation can be achieved with fewer resources.

Big Data

With the large volume of data from all the tools and activities in an organization, big data can be used to optimize the sales organization and address new business challenges.

A sales analytics tool can be used to track historical data, but also used to forecast market trends. For example, does sales increase in a particular pattern that defies seasonality? Or maybe customers only remain loyal for a number of contracts before switching to a competitor? All this can be incorporated into the forecast, and hopefully the negative trends can be reversed.

CPQ data can also be used to track quotations made and actual orders; this would allow the organization to find the sweet spot for pricing each component of future sales. It can be further refined to a region, a country, or a specific segment of customers.

Big data can also be used to determine which products to position in which markets by focusing on customers with the highest propensity who will buy a certain product. This means that we no longer need to build a sales initiative for each customer segment and instead focus on the customers with the highest needs or highest historic demand.

The challenge with big data is that it is difficult to aggregate large amounts of data coming from multiple sources; at times the data is not "clean." This could be due to data being incomplete, inaccurate, or some data could be missing. These issues need to be solved at the source; departments need to be made to understand why sales operations require certain data, and systems may need to be modified to include trackers like customer codes. If the source of the data is external, then the solution becomes a lot more complex to handle.

Data Security

With the huge amount of data that is accessible to sales operations, they are a prime target for security breaches. Customer lists and sales figures are highly confidential and potentially catastrophic if they were to fall into a competitor's hands or into the public domain.

Organizations are starting to enhance the security around such information, and perform regular audits to mitigate threats. Regular password changes, and disabling the accounts of people who leave the company are two simple procedures to assist with this end.

IT Security testing may also be carried out on BI tools and internal systems, to ensure that the systems in place do not have any vulnerabilities.

Sales Operations as a Service

Sales operations as a service is outsourcing the sales operations function, to combine technology with collaborative sales process management. This mitigates the risk of implementing a sales operations function from scratch, by relying on established best practices.

Traditionally, sales performance management software has been the approach to solving problems. However, as we learned in the section on BI tools, software should enable sales and not be implemented just for the latest features. Tools should be combined and integrated into sales processes, as ultimately they have to streamline the sales process.

This is the core benefit of sales operations as a service, as the vendor would have the expertise to enable the sales organization quickly, thus removing the need for trial and error. Of course, fine tuning solutions will still be necessary, but this significantly shortens the time it takes to set up a sales operations function.

Appendix I: Case Study

Why Sales Operations Management Makes a Difference in a Business Organization

Sales Operations Management is no doubt a key part of a business organization. It helps a company improve its sales while lowering sales costs, streamlining the operations processes, and predicting sales targets accurately.

What is Sales Operations Management?

Sales Operations Management is a set of processes and activities that aim to help an organization's sales team run smoothly. They do this to support and fulfill the business's main objectives.

Sales is crucial to any business organization. Sales must be effectively initiated, sustained, created, and continuously monitored in order to achieve better business success. To do all these sales-related activities, the Sales Operations Management arm of a certain business entity moves into action.

What Does Sales Operations Management Address?

To better understand how sales operations management works, take a look at this example:

A certain company X has started expanding its operations overseas. As such, said company has put up new international offices around the globe.

A new sales VP was elected and took office right away. He noticed a few issues that he wants to address as soon as possible. Here are the issues and glitches he aims to fix:

➢ Excessively high cost of sales

There were some sales processes that involved multiple decision makers, and there were some complex ones that had a long turnaround time. All of these processes contributed to the high costs of sales, and the sales VP wanted to find ways to cut these costs.

➢ Inaccurate Sales Activities Forecasting

It was found that the company's salespeople had difficulty in accurately predicting sales forecasts. Different sales managers have varied opinions and meanings to terms such as *engaged, commit,* and *solutioning*.

Also, some salespeople would jump into action first without thinking if the sale would be positive or not. For instance, they would negotiate on details first before product demonstrations, and would propose different solutions first before even qualifying for the sale.

These two things – high sales cost and glitches in forecast accuracy – are important matters that sales operations management hopes to address.

How Does Sales Operations Management Work?

In our example, Company X wants to reduce the high cost of sales operations and improve the accuracy of sales forecasts. Here is how the sales VP uses sales operations management to get these things done:

- Formation of a Sales Operations Team

Creating a new sales operations team is crucial for the success of the sales VP's plans to improve his sales department. This newly formed team will help him create better processes for improving sales, as well as improve sales forecasts across the business.

The sales operations team shall have a sales operations manager, who is tasked to efficiently take the lead in managing client data, establishing adequate and effective sales technologies, helping sales leaders make important decisions, and collaborating with other essential departments within the business entity.

- Decide on an Appropriate Sales Methodology.

Next, the company's sales operations team selects an appropriate sales methodology.

A good sales methodology improves effectiveness of each team member's sales efforts. It can also help foster the development of critical sales skills.

Here is how the company came up with their chosen sales methodology:

- Input from all sales managers were taken. They brainstorm and decide, taking into consideration sales culture and organizational strengths and weaknesses.
- In this case, the company was already a leader in their field. Customers already see their products as a highly trustworthy brand. But they found out that salespersons were unable to secure successful sales because they lacked direct understanding of the customer's main problems (which their products supposedly can address).
- Hence, they decided to use the Solution Selling methodology. This method requires a salesperson to connect with the customer's direct problems and offer the company's products as a way to ease these problems.

Now that they've chosen a methodology, it's time to create a sales process that is aligned to Solution Selling. Here is an example of a sales process fit for Solution Selling methodology:

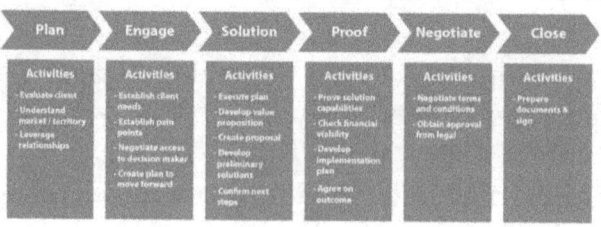

Sales are not dependent on the sales process alone. The company now needs tools to continuously develop their client base and evaluate the effectiveness of their sales efforts through the new methodology. Tools they can use may include CRM and CPQ tools.

- Involving Other Departments in the Sales Operations Efforts

Company X's sales operations team realizes the importance of letting other departments in to better ramp up the effectiveness of their newly-created sales methods and process. Three important departments must join them in their efforts:

> - Marketing – This department holds actual ownership of the product material that salespeople would ultimately sell. They're also involved in generating market leads. Their input is crucial to ensure that sales and marketing will align perfectly in the sales processing tools.
> - IT – Sales processes and tools such as CRM and CPQ are all technologically-advanced. Hence, IT department's involvement is highly required. IT needs to understand the new systems in order to maintain them adequately. Once they know how these systems work, they can already provide support to sales should there be any power outages, hardware problems, or security risks. IT can also incorporate suggestions from salespersons into these tools.
> - Finance – Sales is ultimately about driving company X's revenue up. Hence, Finance department should also be aware of the sales systems. They would clear the budgets for the sales process systems and tools to take

place. They must also understand how sales tools will affect the company's monetary gains in the long run.

- Prepare the systems and let everyone in.

Company X's sales operations team got the systems up, migrated all client data into the new tools, and prepared the training modules for their salespeople.

The team had to slowly but surely incorporate the new systems and tools into salespeople's everyday get-go. They do so by conducting regular training and providing support to salespeople as they try to steer clear from their old sales ways.
- Evaluating lapses and ironing them out.

A new system to be adopted does not always get carried out perfectly in a short span of time. Salespeople need to adjust themselves as they work on using the new systems, CRM and CPQ tools.

Company X's sales operations team actively monitors how their salespeople cope with the new systems. They've identified some difficulties with the new systems, including the following:

> ➢ Salespeople who tend to fall back to their familiar old selling systems.
> ➢ Failing to update the tools after each sales transaction.
> ➢ Feedback from salespersons who were finding it difficult to diagnose customer needs first during a sales engagement.

After identifying these setbacks, Company X's sales operations team develops solutions to help their salespeople effectively cope up with the system changes. Here are some of the solutions they used:

- Identifying team members who had strong knowledge of the current systems, and assigning them as coaches to refresh both sales managers and salespeople about the new systems.
- Refresher courses on the new Solution Selling methodology for managers and salespeople
- Pointing out the necessity and value of CRM and CPQ tools to the success of a sales engagement
- Circulating notes, memos, and newsletters around the company signifying support for the new systems and encouraging all employees to try adapting these systems into their everyday work
- Providing positive reinforcement for salespeople who exhibited proper use of the new systems
- One-to-one coaching sessions for salespeople who are having great difficulty integrating the new system and continue to use their old sales ways
- Accepting feedback from people on the field, and coming up with system tweaks in order to address these feedbacks.

- Continuous evaluation, improvement of systems, and collaboration with other departments

The activities to pursue a new sales process system and incorporate CRM and CPQ tools for the Solution Selling methodology have already spanned a year or so. Company X's sales plans have been carried out, and their salespeople have actively tried out the new systems and are continuously learning the ropes about it.

Compliance to the new sales processes and systems have increased within Company X. Employees and salespersons have seen lots of benefits as they followed the new system. Meanwhile, the sales operations team continuously evaluates the effectiveness of the new systems and adds a few tweaks as they see fit. They also collaborate with other departments to further enhance their sales activities.

The Results of Company X's Sales Operation Management Efforts

In our Company X example, the sales operations team effectively carried out their plans to lessen the cost of sales and improve forecasting of sales activities.

Here are some changes to the Sales Operations Department that Company X saw after adapting their new systems:

- ➤ CRM data showing client records have been cleaned up. Outdated reports were sent to archives, duplicate entries were merged together, and the tools were all updated to show current trends in Company X's sales activities.
- ➤ Reporting tools such as CPQ, contract management, and dashboards were all integrated in the new

system and are constantly being used today. These reporting mediums let sales managers better predict forecasts regarding deals, contracts, and end-sales.

- Basic deals under certain thresholds of volume and revenue were given template contracts for faster approval. Deals qualifying under this need not be passed on to the legal department for creation of individualized contracts, as template contracts were made available to hasten the process of each deal.
- Pre-screened leads were directly passed on from marketing department to the salespeople. This eliminates the need for sales managers to check and approve each lead before passing it on to salespeople. The shortened process allows marketing and sales to actively work together to pre-qualify each lead beforehand.
- Customer engagement were greatly improved with the introduction of CPQ tools. These tools enable salespersons to hasten inquiries with other departments regarding materials, pricing, and other similar information. Hence, the CPQ tools hastened quotation delivery to clients requiring more complex deals.

It is clear that Company X's sales VP have slowly gained his goals of cutting off sales costs and forecasting sales activities in a more accurate manner through his sales operations management efforts.

However, all of these things didn't happen in a quick blink of an eye. The entire sales operations management efforts meant a lot of new work and valuable time spent in creating a new methodology, developing tools aligned with this new method, deploying these tools, training people for the new system, and monitoring compliance and results of these efforts.

Summing It All Up

A company can take steps to improve their sales activities forecasting ad reduce overall sales costs by adapting a sales operations management strategy.

There is no clear-cut rule on how certain companies should adopt sales operations management strategies. It all boils down to the company's individual needs, coupled with their strengths and weaknesses.

Coming up with a good sales methodology, as well as establishing tools to implement it, is a good start to any company looking to further amp up their sales activities. However, developing and implementing this process takes lots of time and effort.

The benefits to creating a sales methodology with tools for implementation clearly outweigh the hard work, efforts, and time spent to get these methods and tools running. Benefits include:

- A streamlined sales process that is uniquely the company's own
- Better forecasting using data management tools like CRM, CPQ, and report dashboards

- Hastening the sales engagement processes in a variety of ways
- Omitting processes that are otherwise lengthening the sales engagement unnecessarily

All these benefits will indeed cut management and sales costs, as well as drive up revenue and increase accuracy of predicting sales activities.

www.ingramcontent.com/pod-product-compliance
Lightning Source LLC
Chambersburg PA
CBHW050240230526
45470CB00005B/2048